11/07

Some Kids Are Blind

Revised and Updated

by Lola M. Schaefer

Consulting Editor: Gail Saunders-Smith, PhD

Consultant: Patricia A. Maurer, Director of Reference
National Federation of the Blind—Jernigan Institute

Capstone
press.

Mankato, Minnesota

Fossil Ridge Public Library District
Braidwood, IL 60408

Pebble Books are published by Capstone Press,
151 Good Counsel Drive, P.O. Box 669, Mankato, Minnesota 56002.
www.capstonepress.com

1 2 3 4 5 6 12 11 10 09 08 07

Library of Congress Cataloging-in-Publication Data
Schaefer, Lola M., 1950–
    Some kids are blind/by Lola M. Schaefer.—Rev. and updated.
    p. cm.—(Pebble books. Understanding differences)
    Includes bibliographical references and index.
    ISBN-13: 978-1-4296-0810-7 (hardcover)
    ISBN-10: 1-4296-0810-2 (hardcover)
    1. Blind children—Juvenile literature. I. Title. II. Series.
HV1596.3.S33 2008
362.40973--dc22   2007009113

Summary: Simple text and photographs describe children who are blind, their
    challenges and adaptations, and their everyday activities.

Note to Parents and Teachers

The Understanding Differences set supports national social studies
standards related to individual development and identity. This book
describes children who are blind and illustrates their special needs.
The photographs support early readers in understanding the text.
The repetition of words and phrases helps early readers learn new
words. This book also introduces early readers to subject-specific
vocabulary words, which are defined in the Glossary. Early readers
may need assistance to read some words and to use the Table of
Contents, Glossary, Read More, Internet Sites, and Index sections
of the book.

Table of Contents

Blindness

Some kids are blind.
Kids who are blind
cannot see.

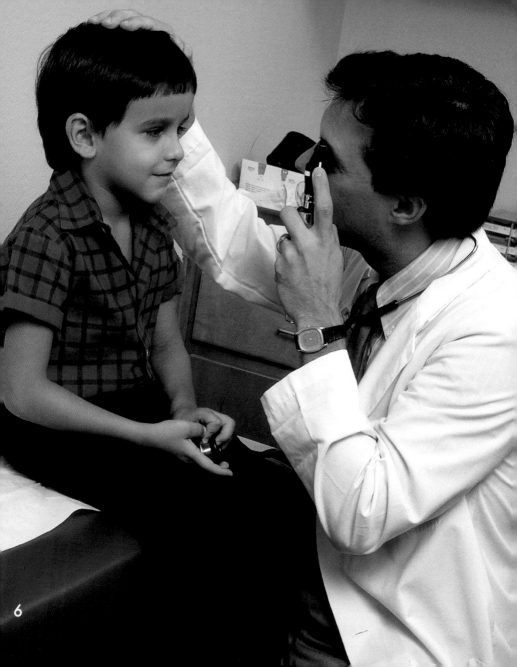

Some kids are blind
when they are born.
Some kids become
blind from a sickness
or from getting hurt.

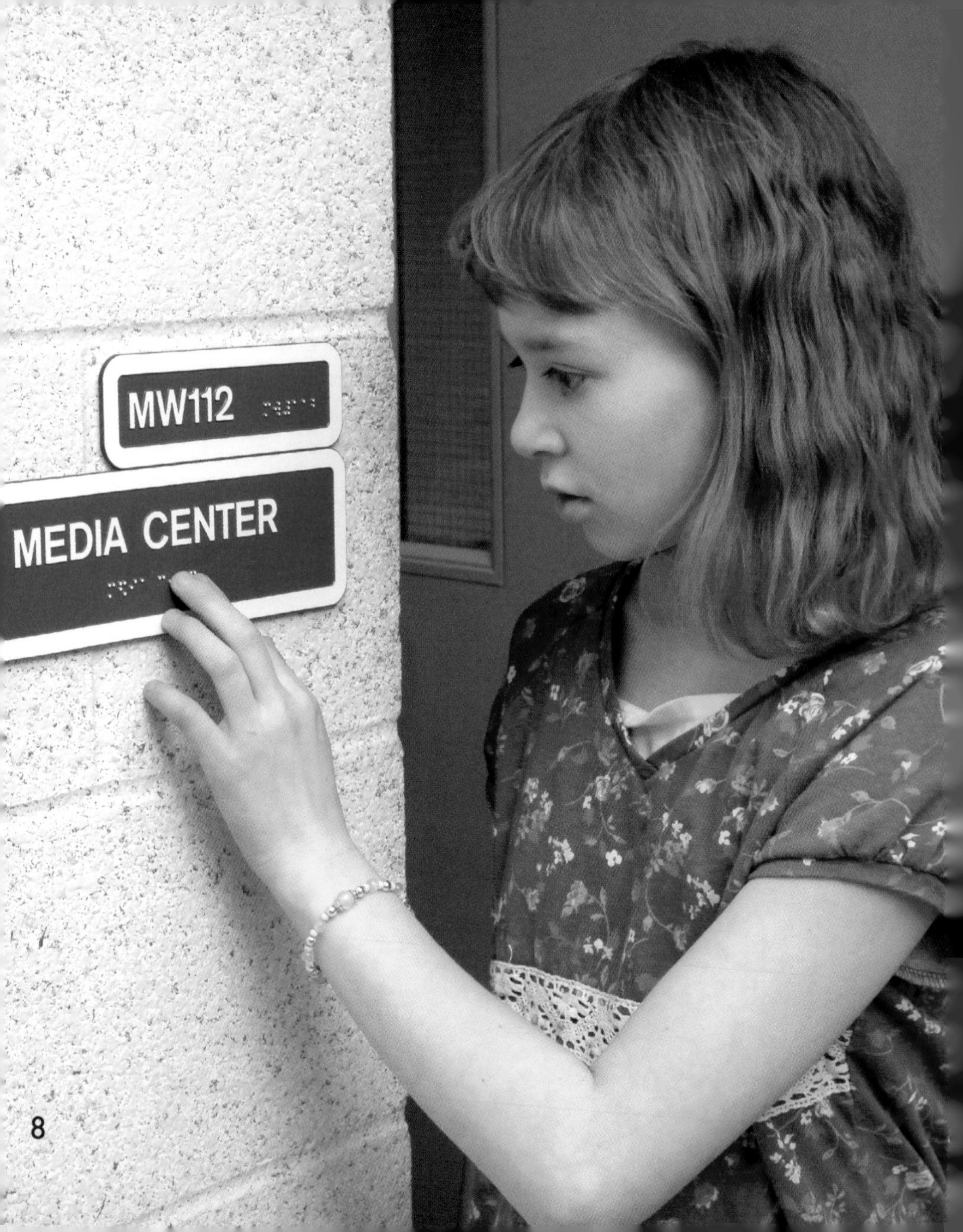
MW112
MEDIA CENTER

Kids who are blind use
their other senses.
They hear their friends
talking on the phone.
They feel things
around them.

Braille

Some kids who are blind
read Braille.
Braille is raised dots
that stand for letters
and numbers.

Some kids who are blind
use Braille notetakers
to do homework
and send e-mail.

Everyday Life

Some kids who are blind
use white canes
to guide them.

Adults who are blind can use guide dogs.

Some kids who are blind enjoy listening to audio books.

Some kids who are blind ride bikes.
They like to have fun.

Glossary

audio book—a recording of someone reading a book aloud

blind—unable to see or having very limited sight; some people who are blind can see light and color.

Braille—a set of raised dots that stand for letters and numbers; people use their fingertips to read the raised dots; Louis Braille of France invented Braille in the early 1800s.

Braille notetaker—an electronic machine that has a Braille keyboard; students can take notes or send e-mail using a Braille notetaker.

guide dog—a dog that is specially trained to lead adults who are blind; guide dogs help adults who are blind move safely in public places.

senses—ways of learning about your surroundings; hearing, smelling, touching, tasting, and seeing are the five senses.

Read More

Jeffrey, Laura S. *All about Braille: Reading by Touch.* Berkeley Heights, NJ: Enslow, 2004.

Patent, Dorothy Hinshaw. *The Right Dog for the Job: Ira's Path from Service Dog to Guide Dog.* New York: Walker & Company, 2004.

Internet Sites

FactHound offers a safe, fun way to find Internet sites related to this book. All of the sites on FactHound have been researched by our staff.

Here's how:

1. Visit *www.facthound.com*

2. Choose your grade level.

3. Type in this book ID **1429608110** for age-appropriate sites. You may also browse subjects by clicking on letters, or by clicking on pictures and words.

4. Click on the **Fetch It** button.

FactHound will fetch the best sites for you!

Index

Word Count: 122
Early-Intervention Level: 10

Editorial Credits
Rebecca Glaser, revised edition edtior; Mari C. Schuh, editor; Bob Lentz, revised
   edition designer; Katy Kudela, photo researcher; Kelly Garvin, photo stylist

Photo Credits
Capstone Press/Karon Dubke, cover, 4, 8, 12, 14, 18, 20
Daemmrich/Pictor, 6
PhotoDisc, Inc., 10
The Seeing Eye, 16

Special thanks to Linda Mitchell, Olda Boubin, Dale Robley, and the students of
Minnesota State Academy for the Blind in Faribault, Minnesota, for their assistance
with photographs for this book.